Design Classics

M

Th

by Carl Jacob Jucker
and Wilhelm Wagenfeld

Verlag form

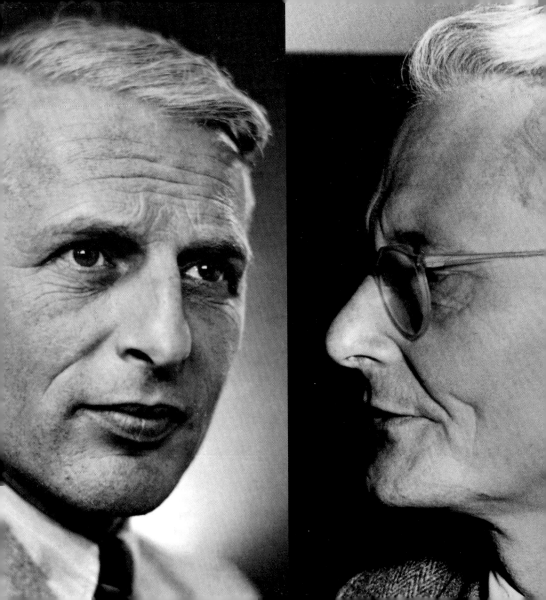

Up to this day, the Bauhaus-lamp is a vivid example of the expectations, the successes and the failures of the Bauhaus-idea. In the manifesto, Principles of Bauhaus Production, Walter Gropius had formulated these principles as follows: "each object," he said, should "fulfill its functions in a practical way and be long-lasting, affordable and beautiful." At the same time, it should be an archetype for industrial production. These principles were not adhered to. The industry couldn't be won over. Still, the lamp remained a symbol of the will of the Bauhaus for modernity; a victory of beautiful appearance and the strong symbolic form over the pure pragmatism of practical utility. Even today, the glass and metal of the reduced naked form volumes are still associated with technology, industry and modernity.

This is even stranger if one thinks of the protean post-war history of lamps and lighting technology. However, the proportions of this Bauhaus-light are so close to an archetype of a table lamp that it has appealed to consumers for decades. The lampshade itself is translucent: it surrounds the light bulb, but it also shines itself. The result is a milky-white light that is bright but not aggressive – as are so many of the extremely luminous low voltage and multi-mirror achievements of the past 15 to 20 years which, although capable of illuminating a private room, tend to confer upon the space the dubious charm of a shop window. The Bauhaus-light is more discrete in this respect: it gives light – for working or living – without placing its users into the spotlight. The moderate hemispheri-cal frosted-glass shade is also a formal archetypal symbol that reminds one of the soft radiance of the moon: technical demands and precise form are thus superimposed on our senses with poetic-literary associations.

Evolution of a New Form Language

It is sensible and important to first be clear about the history of the evolution of this "icon" of form history and design-effect history, since it is as exciting as it is contradictory.

The good-willed consumer is confused at first. Not only does he have the choice between the glass and a metal ver-sions that are offered by the company Tecnolumen under the name Wagenfeld, but he also sees "Bauhaus-lights" that are offered by frequently changing firms from Italy and Spain under the name Carl Jacob Jucker.

Wilhelm Wagenfeld and Carl Jacob Jucker were both gra-duates of Bauhaus, but their lives developed in very different

ways. Jucker (born in 1902 in Zurich, deceased in 1997 in Schaffhausen) worked as a designer in the Swiss silverware factory Jetzler in Schaffhausen for a long time after his time at the Bauhaus, and he also taught. Only because of his Bauhaus lamps – none of them preserved in the original version – is he mentioned in literature. Wagenfeld (born in 1900 in Bremen, deceased in 1990 in Stuttgart) is today considered to be one of the most important German industrial designers. From the 1930s to the '60s there was hardly a household that didn't use one of his glass, metal or plastic products. Numerous awards, exhibitions, publications and now, even a Wilhelm Wagenfeld Foundation in Bremen, honor his consequential decades-long work as a "pattern maker".

Members of the metal workshop of the Bauhaus Weimar, 1925 Seated, from left: Gerhard Vallentin, Laszlo Moholy-Nagy, Wilhelm Wagenfeld, Max Krajewski, Otto Rittweger. Standing: Marianne Brandt, Christian Dell, Josef Knau. Rear: Hans Przyembel

Many publications on the lamp name Jucker/Wagenfeld together, and examination of the specialist literature[1] shows that the Hungarian, Gyula Pap [2], fancied being mentioned as the third participant. In their old age, each of the three proved a claim with such precisely remembered details of the Bauhaus-period that these lucid recollections alone would nip any doubts in the bud if there weren't the obvious contradictions in the statements of the three... Only meticulous research during the past few years has been able to shed light on the complicated history of the evolution of the Bauhaus-light at the Weimar Bauhaus and have separated fact from fiction.

The Bauhaus founded by Walter Gropius in 1919 wanted, as a new school of art, to reform culture in a forward-looking manner. The final goal was the large structure – architecture; but the beginning would be the design of simple household objects. Therefore, there were workshops in textiles, wood, stone, glass, ceramics and metal. Important artists like Paul Klee, Wassily Kandinsky, Johannes Itten, Lyonel Feininger and Oskar Schlemmer taught at the school. During the first expressionist years, basic forms and colors were already a part of the starting point for artistic work. The criticism and influence of the Dutch De Stijl-artists, headed by Theo van Doesburg, effects a reorientation of the Bauhaus from 1922 onward in the sense of modern design. Gropius pragmatically announced in 1922 that the goal was a new symbiosis of art and technology. Now models for industrial production were to be created in the workshops. The metal workshop had been headed by the Hungarian artist Laszlo Moholy-Nagy since the spring of 1923, who, as a theoretician and practician in one, belonged to the Constructivist movement of the time. None of the Bauhaus masters represented Gropius' new course in as engaged a way as Moholy-Nagy. He initiated the work with glass – an unusual material – and, using his own art as a basis, broke the path for a new form language and gave the workshop such contemporary tasks as the designing of lighting appliances.

All of the lamps developed following the impulse of Moholy-Nagy were intended for a very ambitious exhibition project: the sample house "Am Horn" – it still exists today – would demonstrate in an exemplary way modern living and

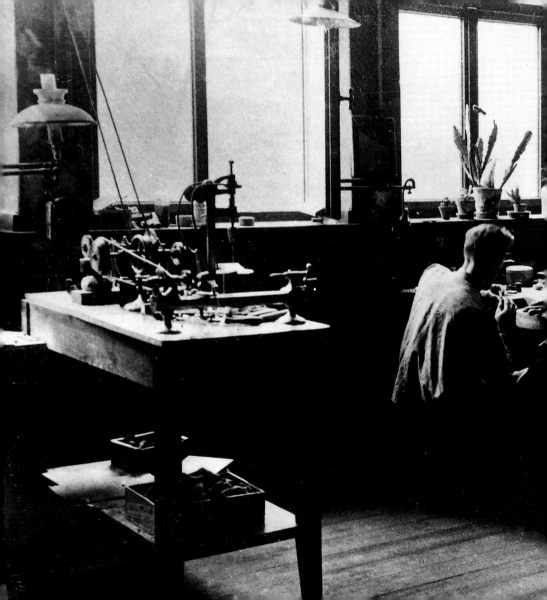

Naum Slutzky in his workshop in Bauhaus Weimar, ca. 1921/22

architecture in 1923. The Swiss, Carl Jacob Jucker, who had just completed his diploma as a silversmith in Zurich, designed various lamps for this house. In two photographs, the Bauhaus documented six of these lamps; each of them had a glass base and a glass shaft and either mirrored bulbs or reflectors. This invention of the glass shaft, within which the electric cable makes the source of energy visible, is a design solution in the spirit of the early Bauhaus. It is Carl Jacob Jucker who deserves the credit for having been the first to design glass table lamps. However, these lamps remained an all-too–conscientious realization of the Bauhaus postulates – in other words: typical students' works. The demonstrative unveiling of all functions resulted neither in better light, nor in convincing designs.

Gyula Pap later claimed that it was he who had placed the glass cylinder onto Jucker's table with the idea of making a lamp with it. He himself had wanted to make a glass samovar with it, but had to leave the Bauhaus before doing so. The work reports from the metal workshop clearly state, however, that Jucker's lamps were finished before Pap left the Bauhaus. Jucker, on the other hand, claimed that he really had intended to add a bell form to his lamp, but that it hadn't arrived in time; so he helped himself out by using a paper shade. But this is also unlikely: if the lamp that he exhibited really wasn't finished, it certainly would not have been photographed at the Bauhaus and published in 1925 in the Bauhaus book *Neue Arbeiten der Bauhaus-Werkstätten* [New Works by the Bau-

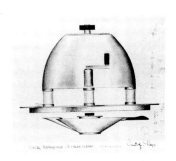

Gyula Pap
Design for an electric tea machine with an extract can made of alpaca and glass, 1923

Opposite: design for an electric tea machine with an extract can made of glass and metal, 1923

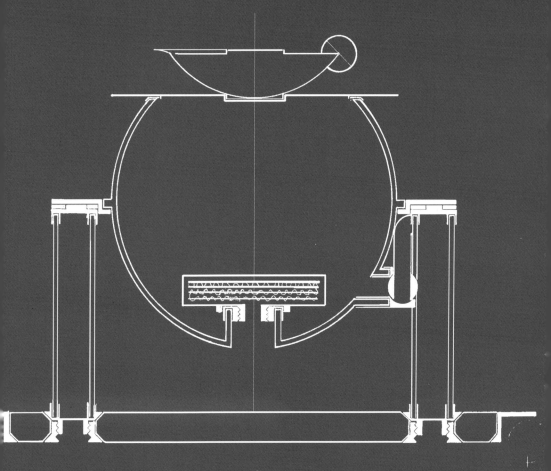

ELEKTR. TEEMASCHIINE   AUS GLAS U. MIETALL   pat. Pap

Modell 1923.

haus-Workshops][3]. Despite the publication, nobody gave any thought to a mass production of this reflector lamp. Jucker left Bauhaus in September 1923 and returned to Switzerland. This means he never had a chance to meet Wilhelm Wagenfeld, who wasn't admitted into the Bauhaus until October 1923. Contrary to Jucker and Pap, Wagenfeld recalled in 1980[4] that Moholy-Nagy had given him the order for a glass lamp after the metal lamp had been finished. Meanwhile, however, it is indisputable that Jucker's glass lamps were completed even before Wagenfeld's arrival at the Bauhaus.

Similar to Jucker, Wagenfeld came to the Bauhaus with a good background education. In his first half-year at the Bauhaus, which was supposed to serve as a preliminary course he was already working in the workshop. And in April 1924 he did his journeyman's exam as a silversmith.

It must have been Moholy-Nagy who urged Wagenfeld to continue working on the theme of the lamp. In March or April of 1924, Wagenfeld developed – analogous to Jucker's glass lamps – a metal lamp with a base plate, a nickel-plated shaft and a frosted glass cupola. Only this lamp, with its calm, floating bell-shape framed by a narrow strip of nickel, met with real approval at the Bauhaus. One of the first lamps was given to Walter Gropius as a birthday present in May of 1924 by the members of the metal workshop.[5] Moholy-Nagy and Gropius found this lamp to be suitable for industrial utilization.

Carl Jacob Jucker
Six variations of table lamps with glass base and glass shaft, 1923

Lighting Apparatus with an Added Esthetic Value

Moholy-Nagy, however, was not satisfied with this design and kept pushing the work further. He suggested equipping Jucker's glass lamp with the glass cupola as well. A short time later, it was probably employees of the wood workshop (turner's workshop) who built crafty versions in wood with fabric or glass shades. Almost at the same time, the glass version was enlarged.

The modular system, according to which substitutions, changes, improvements and enlargements could be made, was considered a kind of key for the rationalization of each design procedure at the Bauhaus. Gropius' architectural office, in which he had developed a "modular kit on a large scale", was first in this effort. But also, the textile and pottery workshops were working with "variations of single components for the factory production".[6] As no one was really familiar with industrial production procedures, it was naively believed that simple "elementary" forms would be especially easy to produce commercially.

Indeed, the production of this lamp could be made only with a high degree of craftsmanship, despite the use of many off-the-shelf products. This "inborn" fault determines the production up to this day. Thus, the Bauhaus-light was a paradox: it looked like a "cheap and practical lighting appliance"[7], but it was actually the result of much-too-expensive manual labor. This had its effect on the price; it was more expensive than lamps offered commercially and therefore

Anonymous, Bauhaus Weimar Table lamps made of wood with fabric and glass shades, 1924.

Opposite: Carl Jacob Jucker, Wilhelm Wagenfeld: Table lamp with glass base, 1924, Gallery Ulrich Fiedler, Cologne.

Next to it is the version enlarged at the Bauhaus Weimar, property of the Bauhaus-Archives Berlin.

never reach the level of mass production that had originally been intended for Bauhaus objects. Besides, the lamp had yet another inherent mistake: the metal workshop dealt with lamps, but not with light. Wagenfeld admitted later on that his first frosted glass cupola was so low that it burst from the trapped heat. In the German lighting industry, the calculation and schematic presentation of the electrical Lux-performance was already common knowledge around 1920; the Bauhaus, however, did not have this knowledge. The master journeyman of the metal workshop, Christian Dell[8], who also was a silversmith, did offer some assistance with this problem; however, the glass cupola of both lamps had to be raised still during the Weimar time. Only years later did Wagenfeld become familiar with the necessary basic know-ledge. So, it wasn't unjust when the ingenious inventor of the Danish PH-lamp, Poul Henningsen[9], sneered at the insufficient lighting appliances in Gropius' proudly published director's room in the avant-garde magazine *Kritisky Revy* in 1924.

These two lamps, which used to belong to Walter and Ilse Gropius, are today in the Busch-Reisinger Museum, Harvard University, Cambridge, Mass.

Almost all of the preserved lamps have different measu-rements and details. In the case of the glass lamps, the dia-meter and height of the glass bases vary considerably in Lucia Moholy's photographs. In Jucker's version, the electric cables were still visible in the glass shaft; in 1924, Wagenfeld moved them into a nickel-plated metal pipe. One year later, he had this improvement patented.[10]

In the metal version, the base – in the beginning a "bur-nished iron plate"[11], meaning a hand-worked plate with a gunmetal finish – was soon replaced by a commercial nickel-plated one. The clear wish for a technical aesthetic is evident in this case.

Around 1924, this "language" of the lamp was considered inappropriate by those who were not friends of the modern era. Its "form image" made it a typical and, at the same time, outstanding product of the Bauhaus around 1923, whose characteristic guiding motifs for form were "the simplest clearest form"[12] and "elementary design". "A round plate[13], a cylindrical pipe and a spherical shade are its most important components," Wagenfeld said in 1924. This strict formalism wasn't very functional, but the lamp was still beautiful. Wagenfeld managed to elevate the object, raising it to the level of archetype through the use of harmonic proportions and a lucky choice of materials; it was even judged to be an "abstract sculpture" (Heyden, 1922).

Wagenfeld attributed to himself with a "feeling for proportional structures".[14] He had said once that he was familiar with how our perception "immediately translates" visual impressions "into light, heavy, very light, very heavy."[15] Carefully designed details such as the three semi-spherical small metal stands on which the base-plate seems to float without seeming to be unstable confirm this claim. Yet another aspect: the nickel border, which seems to carry the glass cupola, mediates for our eye between carrying and loading, light and heavy, floating and holding. Such an added aesthetic value only served to distinguish the best Bauhaus-products

Lucia Moholy photographed the glass and metal version of the Bauhaus-light ca. 1924.

and gave the Bauhaus that radiant force that, up to this day, makes it synonymous with modernism.

So, Wagenfeld created the Bauhaus-light that is still valid today. But his achievement would be unthinkable outside the Bauhaus, i.e., without the preliminary work, the cooperation and the ideas of other Bauhaus-members. Gropius gave the precondition of developing "model handwork" for the industry. Moholy-Nagy suggested building vessels and lighting appliances based on the fusion of basic forms. Gyula Pap was the first to experiment with glass pipes, Jucker built the first glass lamp, Dell took care of the electrical equipment. The balance of this team-performance had to have made a difference: as a form invention, the Bauhaus-light was far ahead of its time. However, its production procedures fell behind the industrial standards and its lighting performance was insufficient.

At this point, the question about the copyright has to be raised at last – and it is disputed up to this day. Should Jucker's glass lamp that was reworked by Wagenfeld carry Jucker's name or Wagenfeld's or both? The Bauhaus itself proceeded here in a non-uniform way and provided the arguments for each of the later parties. What should be done is to follow the modern research and name Jucker/Wagenfeld in connection with the glass lamp, whereas Wagenfeld alone can claim the copyright for the metal version.

Gropius had been considerate enough to assure the copyright to Bauhaus for workshop products, and it could go back to the originator only through specific agreements. The two

Glass version, property of the art collections of Weimar.

lamps were counted among these workshop products. While still in Weimar, the Bauhaus had begun production of the first lamps. And in Dessau, to where Bauhaus had moved in 1925/26, the lamps were produced in the metal workshop from the beginning. Two brochure pages by Herbert Bayer for the newly founded company Bauhaus Inc. document this. As the activities of this new company did not take off as planned, the production of lighting appliances and models was given to the Stuttgart company Paul Stotz. Whether the announced Stotz-catalog was ever published remains doubtful; in July 1928 already, the *Bauhaus-Magazine* published that the Berlin company Schwintzer and Gräff had "taken over 53 Bauhaus-models for lighting appliances for mass production and distribution". Brochures of the Schwintzer & Gräff catalogs show both the large and small Bauhaus-lights. In 1930 at the latest, the Bauhaus again cancelled these contracts. And with this, the production of the lamp by licensees of the Bauhaus was finished.

Mounting ring for the glass cupola from the specimen at Bauhaus-Archives Berlin

Theme with Variations

The mediator for the next chapter of the Bauhaus-light is Dr. Heinrich König. In Dresden, he headed the Architektur-bedarf Ltd. and also distributed products manufactured at Bauhaus. In 1930, he advertised in two brochures for the glass and metal lamp by Wilhelm Wagenfeld. Also in 1930, the magazine Die Form published an advertisement. The legal status of this production is still unclear due to a lack of

gesch.
Höhe ca. 35 cm

AUSFÜHRUNG

Kristallspiegel-Glasplatte, Felsenglasrohr, Glasschirm, Zugfassung

ME
1

TISCHLAMPE AUS GLAS

VORTEILE

1 beste Lichtzerstreuung (genau erprobt)
2 sehr gefällige Form
3 besonders schönes Licht
4 praktisch für Schreibtisch, Nachttisch usw.
5 Glocke festgeschraubt bleibt in jeder Lage unbeweglich

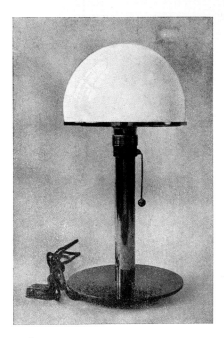

gesch.
Höhe ca. 35 cm
AUSFÜHRUNG

Messing vernickelt, Glasschirm, Zugfassung

ME
2

TISCHLAMPE AUS METALL

VORTEILE

1 beste Lichtzerstreuung (genau erprobt) mit Jenaer Schottglas
2 sehr stabil
3 einfachste, gefällige Form
4 praktisch für Schreibtisch, Nachttisch usw.
5 Glocke festgeschraubt, bleibt in jeder Lage unbeweglich

ARCHITEKTURBEDARF GMBH

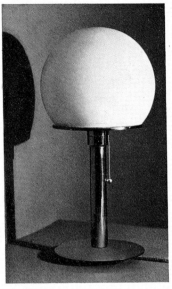

DRESDEN-A.1
WALPURGISSTRASSE 15
TELEFON: 19026
TELEGRAMME: TYPAR

W1

TISCHLEUCHTE

Entwurf: Wagenfeld
Gesetzlich geschützt

RM: 22.—

Gesamthöhe:	38 cm
Fuß: Metall, spritzlack mattschwarz	ø 16 cm
Schaft:	ø 3 cm
Schirm: Milchglas	ø 20 cm
Schirmring:	ø 16 cm

Ausführg. d. blanken Metallteile: messing-vernickelt, poliert

Mattierte Glühlampen vermeiden Schlierenbildungen im Schirm

written documentation. It is not unlikely that Wagenfeld got the copyright from Bauhaus through König's mediation since the Bauhaus, after the cancellation of the contracts with Schwintzer & Gräff, was no longer interested in the production. Back then, Wagenfeld made two copies of the design drawings from 1924.[16] This also could not have happened without permission from the Bauhaus.

From today's perspective, it remains almost incomprehensible how strongly the proportions and the appearance of the lamp had changed. The frosted glass cupola, which was almost a pure hemisphere in the former metal version, now becomes a five-eighths-circle. The round base plate was made smaller, and for the metal version it was painted black at a low cost.

Unfortunately, the Museum of Modern Art in New York shows an example of this top-heavy series with its unbalanced proportions in its design collection. Perhaps 50 of these lamps were produced.[17]

The history of the lamp in post-war Germany started in 1971 when Jucker made a contract with the Italian company Imago for the licensed production of the Bauhaus-light presumably designed by him.[18] However, in Germany it may be offered only as a Jucker-lamp, as the Bauhaus archives had the name "Bauhaus" trademarked. For the past couple of years, the Jucker lamp has been brought onto the market by Spanish producers and, since 1996, another Italian dealer has offered "Bauhaus-lights" by Jucker. However, those who

The preceding pages show two of the brochures designed in 1925 by Herbert Bayer for the „Bauhaus-Katalog der Muster".

Opposite: a brochure page of the Architekturbedarf Ltd. for the metal version redesigned by Wagenfeld, 1930.

7343   1 Lp.

Ausldg. 24 cm
     D.34½ cm
Aluminium, innen
weiss lackiert
Halter Messing,blank-
vernickelt.
rm 120,--

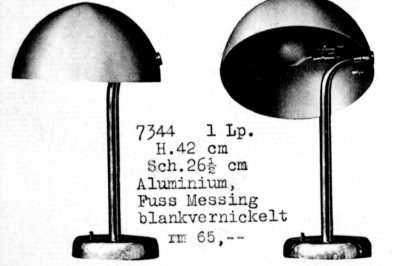

7344   1 Lp.
    H.42 cm
  Sch.26½ cm
Aluminium,
Fuss Messing
blankvernickelt
   rm 65,--

7

o
M
ve
Fu
Ch

Tafel 1708.

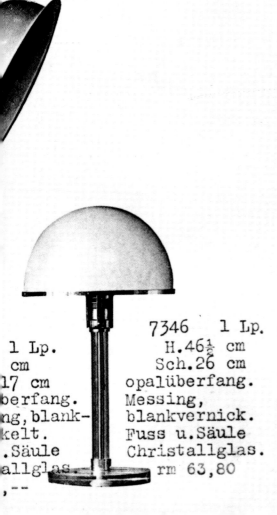

7346   1 Lp.
     H.46½ cm
     Sch.26 cm
opalüberfang.
Messing,
blankvernick.
Fuss u.Säule
Christallglas.
     rm 63,80

1 Lp.
    cm
17 cm
berfang.
ng,blank-
kelt.
.Säule
allglas.
,--

Design for sample page „Bauhaus-Modelle" by Schwintzer & Gräff, Berlin, 1928/29 showing the Bauhaus-light in two sizes.

Wilhelm Wagenfeld
Lamp for Architekturbedarf Ltd.,
Dresden, 1930

Opposite: Re-edition against original: Wagenfeld's re-edited lamp for Tecnolumen, 1980, and an old version.

The following pages show on the left, a Jucker-lamp from the Italian production during the '70s, next to an old version of the Bauhaus-light, and on the right, the lamp re-edited by Wagenfeld for Tecnolumen, next to an old version.

compare these Jucker-lamps with the old Bauhaus-light will turn away in disappointment: rough proportions and the awkward cupola of this plagiarism insults the eye.

In 1980 the Bremen company Tecnolumen in cooperation with Wilhelm Wagenfeld put a new edition of his metal lamp from 1924 onto the market.[19] The cupola was minimally raised, the base received a smaller diameter, its plate thickness was reduced and the entire lamp became more gracious. Wagenfeld's new edition softened and disciplined the expressive value of the strong details, which still provided sculptural qualities and, in the end, turned the lamp into a pleasing design object. A short time later, Tecnolumen also brought the glass lamp redesigned by Wagenfeld onto the market. Both lamps are offered only under the name of Wagenfeld – a decision that would be forbidden according to today's knowledge about the history of the lamp's evolution. The metal pull chain copied from the early lamps had to be replaced by a plastic cord according to German VDE regulations.[20]

Dialectics of Tradition and Modernism

Klaus-Jürgen Sembach has pointed out that it was the traditional reversions especially that made the Bauhaus-light such a success.[21] Wagenfeld did not want to make everything new and different at any price, but had reverted to familiar forms. These familiar forms go way back into the 19th century. At the beginning of the type sequence stands the Biedermeier oil lamp, which can be seen in an 1830 portrait by the Swabian

Unternehmenslustige Finanzierungs-vermittler aus gutem Hause zwecks dauerhafter Partner-schaft gesucht.

Die L-Bank bietet Finanzierungs-vermittlern Kapital für ihre Kunden zu günstigen Konditionen.

Sie haben Kunden mit Kapitalbedarf und suchen einen erfahrenen Finanz-partner? Dann sind Sie bei der L-Bank an der richtigen Adresse. Denn die L-Bank bietet Ihren Kunden gutes Geld.

Und das heißt, gute Konditionen, die für den gesamten Finanzierungsrahmen gelten. Mit der Möglichkeit, die Zinsen langfristig festzuschreiben und den Anteil der Tilgung gemäß den Wün-

schen Ihrer Kunden fes[...] zählen für die kompete[...] berater der L-Bank nic[...] und Zinsen. Mit Sachk[...] und langjährigen Erfah[...]

Leonhardt & Kern

For the uninitiated, even the rough Jucker-version becomes the icon of Modernism. Advertisement for a bank, 1996.

Immobilienfinanzierung schaffen sie die Grundlage für eine erfolgreiche Zusammenarbeit. Und eine dauerhafte Partnerschaft. L-Bank, Schloßplatz 10/12, 76113 Karlsruhe Telefon 0721/150-0.

L-BANK
Landeskreditbank Baden-Württemberg

Leistung und ein Lächeln.

Top: „My room Weimar" was what the Bauhaus student Paul Citroen called this drawing.
Bottom: Richard Riemerschmid: table petroleum lamp, before 1910.

Opposite: Franz Seraph Stirnbrand painted the actor Karl Seydelmann ca. 1830, in the background, an oil lamp.

painter Stirnbrand. A petroleum lamp designed by Riemerschmid shows the type during the time of German Art Nouveau. Even in the metal workshop of the Bauhaus, a movable wall lamp – probably gas – of this type with a light shade framed by a metal border could be found. When the first electric table lamps were designed around 1900, the glass cupolas, which up to then had always been pierced by a cylinder, were closed.

In the circle of the Vienna workshops we encounter strictly geometric, stylized lamps by Adolf Loos and Josef Hoffmann of which only very few examples were produced. During this time, we also find the first glass lamp shafts that Jucker fell back on.

In Germany, Bruno Paul translated the type again into an agreeable form. Wagenfeld – consciously or unconsciously – continued the tradition of this type. He modernized it radically in the sense of a new Bauhaus aesthetic, thus signaling a change in the paradigm from Art Nouveau to Neo-Functionalism. The cool nickel replaced the warmer brass that had been the norm up to then, and the elementary forms were the messengers of a machine aesthetic.

In the twenties, there were already a series of blatant copies, such as those by the Bauhaus-student Franz Singer or the translations into a different material like those by Karl Müller, Burg Giebichenstein and Halle. Plagiarisms of the Bauhaus-light came onto the market from Bünte & Remmler, Frankfurt, and from Brendel, Berlin. Their archetype, however,

Predecessors and followers:
Upper row from left:
Josef Hoffmann, table lamp, 1904.
Anonymous, Vienna Workshops, table lamp, brass, around 1902/03
Table lamp made of glass and brass, Vienna, 1902.
Bottom row from left:
Candle stick with glass shaft, 1902
Bruno Paul, table lamp, 1901/04
Franz Singer, table lamp, around 1928

was possibly the version from Architekturbedarf, Dresden. Christian Dell, the former head of the metal workshop in Weimar, tried to solve the basic problem of the Bauhaus-light in 1928, which was: "that the maximum lighting is on the lamp's base."[22] His smart lamp with a reflector that he created as a teacher at the Frankfurt School of Art couldn't correct this "basic evil", either.

Who actually used the lamp during the twenties? We see it most frequently on Bauhaus-photographs. Walter Gropius set them up in his office and apartment. The Moholy-Nagy couple had it in Madam's bedroom in their master house in Dessau in 1927.

The architect Bruno Taut put it – like Gropius – onto his own desk. The architects Franz Schuster, Grete Schütte-Lihotzky and Ferdinand Kramer exhibited it in model apartments designed for the low-income families in Frankfurt. But even the more conservative Adolf G. Schneck include the lamp as part of the furnishings of an apartment and it can even be found in the Vienna Villa Steiner by Adolf Loos.

Contrary to this, the Bauhaus-directors Hannes Meyer and Mies van der Rohe didn't like the lamp. Meyer preferred the lights by Zeiss-Ikon and van der Rohe used the above-mentioned PH-Lamps almost exclusively.

During the twenties, the Bauhaus-light had already come under the shadow of a lighting fashion that slowly unfolded from 1925 onward. The interest was directed increasingly towards the swivel and mobile lamps that were being mass-produced by many companies for offices and workspaces.

Christian Dell: "Vollkugel-Tisch-lampe" (full sphere table lamp) with a rotating "metal-light-pro-tector", prototype, 1928

Mounting of different lamps around 1930. Picture 2 shows a plagiarism of the Bauhaus-light by Bünte and Remmler, picture 4, a lamp by Wagenfeld, picture 5, a lamp by Franz Müller from the workshops of the city of Halle, designed 1926/27.

Every manufacturer delivered, at no cost to their customers, diagrams and lighting curves for proof of functionality. Bauhaus joined this development with its designs for Kandem-lamps in 1928, thereby also entering the private home.

There is no documentation for an international distribution of the lamp during the years of the Weimar Republic. Moholy-Nagy did exhibit it during the show of the German Werkbund in 1930 in Paris, but the most important French collection Le Luminaire[23] had passed up this and other important achievements out of "total ignorance" – these are the words of the new publisher in 1992.

Only today has the lamp gained a secure place in all reference works on the history of lighting appliances [24], whether English, Dutch or German. How thoroughly the original had been forgotten in Germany after 1945 became clear in 1980, when a plagiarism of the lamp from the Limburg glass works received an award for "good industrial form" during the Hannover Fair.[25] Two years later the "real" Tecnolumen metal lamp by Wagenfeld would win the Federal Prize "Good Form" by the Council for Design in Frankfurt. Up to the present, the glass version has always sold noticeably better than the metal version.

Strangely enough, the ubiquitous presence of replicas has had a clear effect on our picture of the Bauhaus over the past few years. The lamp may have been present as a museum piece at every important Bauhaus-exhibition, but only in recent years has it been celebrated by the press and art dea-

Gregotti, Meneghetti, Stoppino: *Bina* lamp, producer Candle, 1963

Opposite: For the "Neues Frankfurt", Ferdinand Kramer designed this combination furniture in 1928, which he decorated with the Bauhaus-light.

Still available today: plagiarisms of the Bauhaus-light from the glass works Limburg.

Following page: Interior of the Ludwig Grote apartment, Dessau, by Marcel Breuer, 1927.

lers as "conclusive, without frills and beautiful," and as one of the "most famous objects from the Bauhaus."[26] Thus, the "simple lamp" became a "star" in its second life.

Acknowledgments

I would like to thank Beate Manske, Wagenfeld Foundation, Bremen; Walter Schnepel, Tecnolumen, Bremen and Wolfgang Werner, Bremen for the information they provided. I would also like to thank my colleagues Peter Hahn and Klaus Weber in the Bauhaus-Archives Berlin, for their advice and help. Thanks also to Eckard Neumann and Volker Fischer, Frankfurt/Main, and to Ulrich Fiedler, Cologne, who provided me with an illustration. My special thanks go to Winfried Nerdinger and Manfred Ludewig for their constructive criticism.

Notes

1 Thomas Heyden: *Die Bauhauslampe. Zur Karriere eines Klassikers*, Berlin 1992 (Bauhaus-archives, Museumspädagogischer Dienst, Berlin. Series: Gegenwart Museum). Beate Manske: "Zwei Lampen sind nie gleich. Wilhelm Wagenfeld in der Metallwerkstatt des Staatlichen Bauhauses Weimar", in: *Die Metallwerkstatt am Bauhaus*. Exhibition catalog Bauhaus-Archives Berlin. Edited for the Bauhaus-archives by Klaus Weber, Berlin 1992, pp 79-91.
Klaus Weber: "Vom Weinkrug zur Leuchte. Die Metallwerkstatt am Bauhaus", in: *Die Metallwerkstatt am Bauhaus*, pp. 9-41. Klaus Weber: "Carl J. Jucker und Wilhelm Wagenfeld, Tischlampe, 1923/24," in: Exhibition catalog *Experiment Bauhaus*, Berlin 1988, p 136. Christian Wolsdorff: "Die Bauhauslampe - Versuch einer Rekonstruktion ihrer Entstehungsgeschichte", in: *Design - Formgebung für jedermann, Typen und Prototypen*, exhibition catalog, Zurich, Kunstgewerbemuseum, 1983, pp. 48-55.
Christian Wolsdorff: "Designer im Widerspruch," in: *md Möbel interior design*, issue 4, 1984, pp 27-30.
2 Gyula Pap: "Zur Entwicklung der Jucker-Wagenfeld-Tischlampe", in: *bauhaus 3*, catalog of the Galerie am Sachsenplatz, Leipzig 1978, pp 15.
Hubertus Gaßner: "Zwischen den Stühlen sitzend sich im Kreise drehen, Marcel Breuer und Gyula Pap als Bauhaus-Gestalter," in: *Wechselwirkungen, Ungarische Avantgarde in der Weimarer Republik*, exhibition catalog, Kassel 1986, pp 312-328.
3 Neue Arbeiten der Bauhauswerkstätten. Published by Hans M. Wingler. New series of the Bauhaus books initiated by Walter Gropius and Laszlo Moholy-Nagy, Mainz and Berlin 1981, (Reprint Bauhaus books Vol. 7).
4 Wilhelm Wagenfeld, "Bauhaus-Glaslampe, 1980", in: *Glaslampe 1924*, brochure of Tecnolumen company, Bremen 1980, no page.

5 Weber (Vom Weinkrug...) op. cit., footnote 1: here a verse for Gropius is quoted which can only refer to the Bauhaus-light: "Was wäre die All-Werkstatt/Ohne die Metall-Werkstatt/Was das Theater ohne Rampe/Was das Licht ohne eine Lampe/Deshalb bauten wir aus Glas/Nickelblech und sonst noch was/Aus Konstruktivistischer Fülle/Diesem Licht da eine Hülle/Unserem Gropius Walter/Mög' es leuchten bis ins Alter." [What's the studio aggregate/Without the metal workshop as its mate/The theatre without a ramp/Or the light without a lamp/So we took the precious glass/Nickel sheets and other mass/And out of Constructivist wealth and pride/A shell for this light we built and tried/To Walter Gropius our brilliant sage/May it shine until his oldest age]

6 "Bauhaus Weimar", special edition of the magazine *Junge Menschen*. Kraus Reprint, Munich 1980, pp 171-172

7 Josef Albers: "Werkstattarbeiten des Staatlichen Bauhauses zu Weimar", in: *Das badische Handwerk 1925*, Karlsruhe 1925, pp 3-9, here: p 9.

8 Christian Dell: *Silberschmied und Leuchtengestalter im 20. Jahrhundert*. Exhibition catalog Museum Hanau, Philippsruhe castle 1996.
Idee Christian Dell. Einfache, zweckmäßige Arbeitsleuchten aus Neheim. Exhibition Amsberg-Sundem 1995. Edited by Peter M. Kleine and Klaus Struve).

9 *Light Years Ahead. The Story of the PH Lamp*. Edited by Tina Jorstian and Poul Erik Munk Nielsen, Copenhagen 1994.

10 *Täglich in der Hand. Industrieformen von Wilhelm Wagenfeld aus 6 Jahrhunderten*. Edited by Beate Manske and Gudrun Scholz, Bremen 1987.

11 *Neue Arbeiten* op. cit. p 69

12 *Junge Menschen* op. cit. p 171

13 *Junge Menschen* op. cit. p 182

14 Wilhelm Wagenfeld: "Die Geschichte meiner Bauhauslampe...", 1980, in: *Bauhauslampe 1924* op. cit.

15 Wagenfeld, "Geschichte..." op. cit.

16 Illustration of a copy, in: *Bauhaus Utopien. Arbeiten auf Papier*. Edited by Wulf Herzogenrath. Exhibition catalog, Cologne 1988, p 137

17 Wagenfeld, "Glaslampe" op. cit.

18 Daniele Baroni: C. J. Jucker. *The lamps 1923-24.*Special print by Tlopi, (House publication of Imago, Milano, n.d. (1982?) Milan.

19 Wagenfeld interview, *Antiquitäten-Zeitung*, 1980, no. 8, p 167 and 1980, no. 9, p 198

20 Kind information by Walter Schnepel, Bremen

21 Klaus-Jürgen Sembach: "Über die Tischlampe von Wilhelm Wagenfeld und Karl J. Jucker," in: Manske, Beate / Scholz, Gudrun (ed.): *Täglich in der Hand*, op. cit., p 228.

22 Wilhelm Lotz (ed.), *Licht und Beleuchtung*, Berlin 1928, p 24

23 Guillaume Janneau: *Le Luminaire Art deco Lampen 1925-1937*, Stuttgart

1992, p 23.

24 Andre Koch: *Struck by lighting. An art historical introduction to electrical lighting design for the domestic interior*, Rotterdam 1992
Daniele Baroni: *L'oggetto Lampada. Forma e Funzione,* Milan 1981. *Bei Licht besehen. Kleines ABC der Beleuchtung*, Gummersbach 1987 (Schriften des Rheinischen Museumsamtes no. 389).Wolfgang Schivelbusch: *Licht, Schein und Wahn. Auftritte der elektrischen Beleuchtung im 20. Jahrhundert*. Lüdenscheid 1992.

25 "Im Schatten von Bauhaus", in: *Antiquitäten-Zeitung* 1980, no. 11, p

24 "Schlüssig, schnörkellos...", in: *Art*, Hamburg, issue 6, 1986

26 Diary Ilse Gropius, 1924

Photo Credits

pp 4,28: Wilhelm Wagenfeld Stiftung, Bremen; pp 7, 8: Bauhaus-Archiv, Berlin, photo: Lepkowski; p 11: Bauhaus-Archiv Berlin, photo: Jost Schilgen; pp 18, 23: Bauhaus-Archiv Berlin, photo: Lucia Moholy; pp 12/13, 16: Bauhaus-Universität, Weimar; pp 14/15: Iparmüveszeti Museum Budapest, photo: Richard Wagner; p 19: Galerie Ulrich Fiedler, Köln (l.), photo: Andreas Jung, Düsseldorf; pp 20, 21: Courtesy of the Busch-Reisinger Museum Harvard; p.24: Kunstsammlungen zu Weimar; p. 25, 26, 27, 30, 31, 38 (a.): Bauhaus-Archiv Berlin; p 32: Museum of Modern Art, New York; pp 23, 24, 25, 41 (b.): Bauhaus-Archiv Berlin, photo: Hans-Joachim Bartsch; pp 36, 37, 42, 45: Ludwig Neundörfer, *So wollen wir wohnen*, Stuttgart 1931; p 38 (b.) Bauhaus-Archiv Berlin, from Klaus Peter Arnold: *Vom Sofakissen zum Städtebau. Die Geschichte der deutschen Werkstätten*, Dresden/Basel 1993; p 39: Kunsthalle Bremen; p 40: (a.l.) Archiv der Wiener Werkstätten; (a.r.) Katalog Fischer Fine Art, London 1979; (b.l.) Hochschule für angewandte Kunst, Wien; (b.r.) Alfred Ziffer, Bruno Paul, exhibition catalog München 1992; p 41 (a.): Hochschule für Angewandte Kunst; p 43: Sandor Dell; p 46: Limburger Glashütte; p 49: Bauhaus-Archiv Berlin, Erich Consemüller.

Service

If you would like to receive our catalog,
please contact us:
Verlag form. Books & Magazines on
design issues.
Telephone: 49 (0) 69 94 33 25-0
Facsimile: 49 (0) 69 94 33 25-25

Impressum

©1997 Verlag form GmbH,
Frankfurt am Main
All rights reserved, especially those of
translation into other languages.

Translated into English by:
Katja Steiner and Bruce Almberg

Graphic design:
Sarah Dorkenwald, Andreas Liedtke
Absatz, Gesellschaft für Kommuni-
kations-Design, Frankfurt am Main

Lithography:
Druckagentur Robert Eichhorn,
Frankfurt am Main

Print:
Gotha Druck und Verpackung
GmbH & Co. KG, Wechmar

Die Deutsche Bibliothek - CIP-Einheits-
aufnahme

Droste, Magdalena:
The Bauhaus light by Carl Jacob Jucker
and Wilhelm Wagenfeld / Magdalena
Droste. (Aus dem Dt. von Katja Steiner
und Bruce Almberg). - Frankfurt am
Main : Verl. Form, 1997
(Design classics ; 8)
Dt. Ausg. u.d.T.: Droste, Magdalena:
Die Bauhaus-Leuchte von Carl Jacob
Jucker und Wilhelm Wagenfeld

ISBN 3-931317-47-1